Mandela

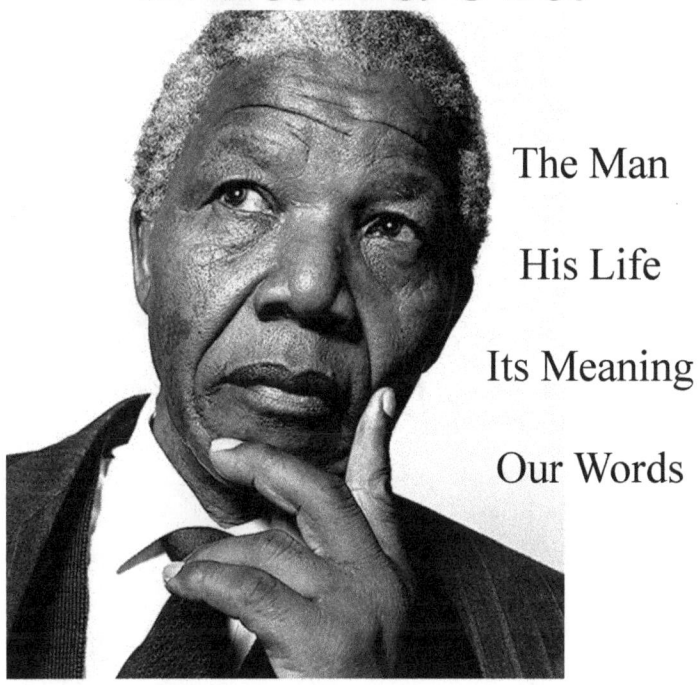

The Man

His Life

Its Meaning

Our Words

Poetry . . . Commentary & Stories
The Anthological Writers

inner child press, ltd.

Credits

Concept
Inner Child

Compiled by
Janet P. Caldwell

Foreword
Robert Gibbons

Preface
William S. Peters, Sr.

Cover
Inner Child Press, ltd.

General Information

Mandela

The Anthological Writers

1st Edition : 2014

This Publishing is protected under Copyright Law as a "Collection". All rights for all submissions are retained by the Individual Author and or Artist. No part of this Publishing may be Reproduced, Transferred in any manner without the prior **WRITTEN CONSENT** of the "Material Owner" or its Representative Inner Child Press, ltd.. Any such violation infringes upon the Creative and Intellectual Property of the Owner pursuant to International and Federal Copyright Law. Any queries pertaining to this "Collection" should be addressed to Publisher of Record.

Publisher Information
1st Edition : Inner Child Press :
intouch@innerchildpress.com
www.innerchildpress.com

This Collection is protected under U.S. and International Copyright Laws

Copyright © 2014 : The Anthological Writers

ISBN-13 : 978-0615968230 (Inner Child Press, Ltd.)
ISBN-10 : 0615968236

$ 12.95

Dedication

Truth

Parity

Progress

Harmony

Humanity

Love

Preface

We at Inner Child Press believe in the Power of the Written Word. What better use can we apply our Thoughts, Spirits and Love to than to commemorate the works of such a significant soul as Nelson Mandela aka Madiba.

This man has suffered much for the parity of his people, all people which translates into the equality of all Human Beings upon the planet. Our words will preserve the Life for those yet unborne and educate those amongst us who know not of his Humanitarian efforts and impact.

In this wonderful coming together of Poets and Writers we offer you our humble perspectives and hope that you find our words significant to your own consciousness, not only of Mr. Nelson Mandela aka Madiba, but that of Self and all members of Humanity.

Bless Up

Bill

Inner Child
www.iaminnerchild.com
www.innerchildpress.com

Foreword by Robert Gibbons

" I was fighting because I wanted to say, I am African. This is my country, you are not going to oppress me in my own country"

~ for Nelson Mandela

"Now come, you, House of Xhosa, I give you the Morning Star because it is the most important star, the star for counting the years, the years of manhood." (Mqhayi, poet of the Xhosa people)!

When the editors of this press approached me about writing the forward for this anthology I immediately became intimidated. How could I write a fresh take on one of the most documented men in the world? After his transition to the ranks of ancestors; some of the headlines come to mind:

1. The Mandela I Knew (New York Times)
2. Let him go, doctors urge Nelson's family (Daily News)
3. Mandela's Death Leave South Africa without a Moral Center (New York Times)
4. Where Mandela Kept Hope, Guides Tell Their Shared Saga (New York Times)

Even though Nelson Mandela received day to day press coverage during his lifetime the closest I ever came to Mandela was the appearance of Dennis Brutus in New York before his death. " Brutus was arrested in 1960 for breaking the terms of his banning which he could not meet more than two people outside his family, and sentences to 18 months in jail. However he jumped bail and fled to Mozambique where Portuguese secret police arrested him and returned him to South Africa. There while trying to escape, he was shot in the back at point black range. After partly recovering from the wound, Brutus was sent to

Robben Island for 16 months, five in solitary. He was in a cell next to Nelson Mandela." (Wikipedia)

To hear Brutus read some of his poems was a historic event. For those of us that never had a chance to witness a man who fought for equality all of his life. I think Derek Walcott was correct when he said, "the chronicler, the recorder, the diarist, writing of new and unexplored world." (the Art of Derek Walcott) I think the stories in between the press coverage and the newspaper articles are just as important. We get a sense that these are real individuals, not some myth we have created in our heads. Often times we are so inundated with social media that we lose the sense of the struggle of these individual warriors. Brutus had his share of struggle, but he endured.

> This is one of my favorite poems by Brutus:
>
> if in fact it is all we shall know
> as indeed may be most probable
> and if as is reasonably certain
> we shall have no more on earth
> then it is wrong to lament
>
> (Dennis Brutus)

If it is wrong to lament then this should not be about biography or myth making, but how can I as an American; a colonial brother use the life and legacy of iconic figures such as Mandela and Brutus to understand the world we live in. Brutus was a traveler figure. He was an outsider, a detached observer after seeking asylum in London and then the United States. He wanted to tell his story in his own voice. This is what we must do, in my opinion, tell our own story in our voice. If Walcott is correct when he reports to us how we must forge language and memory. "It culminates into an image of sacrificial burning; the artist is released from his clay prison by the fires of inspiration."

(the Art of Derek Walcott) "wrong to wish for the end of life wrong to feel one must drag somehow through ad surely one must fill each day with living and do each day as much as we can" (Dennis Brutus)

If Mandela and Brutus sacrificed their entire lives for the cause of injustice, then how do we fit into the equation and what can be done to extend the legacy, if memory can sometimes be inconvenient and unreliable. To chronicle a man more iconic that President Obama or Frederick Douglass; to be a powerful witness to his legacy; to use the term loosely within the parameters of aesthetic distance. I am studied, cultured, and cosmopolitan. I should know Nelson Mandela. I should be able to track his years as a father, barrister, President, grandfather, icon, and now ancestor, but me, like many colonial brothers that are weaned from the diaspora; that have never set foot on African soil; never had the primacy of African culture, or the experience of a rites of passage; nor know the importance of oral tradition. The griot. The paramount chief. Never being privy to our ancestral biography it becomes complicated. We become conflicted that our lives are so torn. We become as lost as the middle passage. We contend that it does not relate to us. Reclaiming this heritage is not a part of our immediate agenda. So we seek solace in the immediate. We live in a romanticized version of it during Black History Month or during the killing of another man of color. The Basil Davidson version. The version we saw as youngster sitting in front of our comfortable televisions. Viewing African culture is distant from us. Living as separate as the white man that brought us here or the king that sold us. We are still benighted within ourselves. Clutching to some syncretic survivalism in style, in tongue, in church, in food, or vernacular. Because we do not understand the importance of reclaiming this history. We become a creation of a creation-shedding the original, forgetting lineage. Our background has been assassinated. That America is my motherland and my fatherland, until I am educated in the truth.

But what about the brothers and sister that will never receive correction? It survives, too.I can not compete with the great biographers of this age. But, because I can not compete with the great biographers whether because of name recognition or credentials does not mean I can not have my sanfoka moment. It does not mean I can not look back diachronically and synchronically at this history. To those who have gone before me. The men and women that fought the good fight. This is reason I write these words.

As Mandela lay in state in our national consciousness he is reported to have transitioned at 8:50 p.m. local time. He will be buried in the village of Qunu. A village where three of his exhumed children was interred earlier in 2013. We reach back to the beginning-to our beginning. The blood stain of history. The legacy and the peculiar institutions of the old and new regimes. we savor the moments as we mature. And we understand finally that the underground becomes the utmost. The last shall be first. The crowds that came to memorialize him chanted:

> Ngawethu (Power shall be ours)
> Mayibuye, iAfrika (Come back Africa)
> Batebegiyi (Those who die dancing)
> Nkosi SiKelel' iAfrika (God bless Africa)
> Andizi ndisaqula (I will not come, I am girding for battle)

Yes, we die dancing. We cry for our lands. Our landless and our landlocked mentalities. And we understand now he is being brought up here. We can no longer ask. We must act in the present. In that great getting up morning. In that great underground mission to glory full of warriors and warrior-womyn, conjurers, saints, elders, and ancestors. The heaven is full of Harriet, Denmark, Touissant, Nat, Frederick, Nkrumah, Sisulu, and Martin. We are free. No longer arrested. No longer illegal. No longer colonial, but we remember the words of Winnie when she said, "part of my soul went with him." All the quotes and salutations and benedictions making him ready for sainthood. He will robe again in traditional Thembu costume known as the kaross. In which he wore on Earth before his ascension. the skins of jackals at an angle to expose his holy shoulder. Because we stand on the shoulders of our ancestors. He will wear traditional beads around his neck and legs because he is not Zulu, he is Xhosa.

We come back to the words of Walcott and Mqhayi:

> 1. maturity is the assimilation of the features of every ancestor
> 2. if the writer is to grow he must go beyond the confrontation of history
> 3. it is therefore become necessary for the writer to make repeated, unending,
>   exploration of the same territory since every journey throw up new truths.

Let me die dancing. Let me chant their names internally and eternally. Let me remain here until the great getting up morning when I was only colonial. I was only history. I was only mimetic. In fact, I am merely pre-dawn-sharing half dark-half light. But now, To answer Countee Cullen famous question especially for him: What is Africa to me? And the answer would be: I am among the stars, because this is how one sunrise.

Robert Gibbons

New York City, 2014

Robert Gibbons

Robert Gibbons Bio

Robert Gibbons is originally from Belle Glade (Palm Beach County), Florida. He is the oldest of five children from a Palm Beach County elementary school teacher of more than thirty years. An honor graduate of Glades Central High School, Robert matriculated to Florida A&M University in Tallahassee, Florida, where he received the B.S. in History in 1989. Robert has taught in the Palm Beach County School District; the Prince George's County School District; the Fairfax County School District; and now works as an English Specialist for the Renaissance Charter High School of Innovation of East Harlem (Manhattan), New York City.

Robert Gibbons moved to New York City in the summer of 2007 in search of his muse-Langston Hughes. Robert has featured in many venues around New York City. Not only in New York City, but also in Washington, D.C. ;
Maryland, and Florida. He most recently has offered his poetic performances in such places as: Cornelia Street Café; the Church of the Village; the Saturn Series; Perch Café; Barnes and Nobles Brooklyn; the Saturn Series; Stark Performances; Otto's Shrunken Head; Poets on White; Nomad's Choir; Taza de Café and many others. Moreover, Robert has been published in Uphook Press; Three Rooms Press; Stain Sheets; Brownstone Anthology; Dinner with the Muse; Cartier Street

Review; Nomad's Choir; Palm Beach Post; and recently was produced on CD called Brain Ampin through Hydrogen Jukebox, a poetry series produced through the Cornelia Street Café. Additionally, Robert has taken classes with Cave Canem and the 92Y and has studied under master poets such as: Cornelius Eady, Marilyn Nelson, KImiko Hahn, Nathalie Handal, Linda Susan Jackson, Kevin Young and Kwame Dawes.

Robert Gibbons has done other poetic works in after school programs, drama camps, and theater programs in Florida, Washington, D.C., and New York City. He hopes to continue searching to find new ways to create work and

provide new venues to the children he serves. Robert just released his first collection poetry published by Three Rooms Press, Close to the Tree.

Table of Contents

The Words

Vensan Kamberk	1
Deryn de Temple	3
Kolade Olanrewaju Freedom	8
Anthony Arnold	11
Intricate B aka Jason Brierly	15
Sue Lobo	17
Lanaia Lee	21
Steve Brightman	23
Anthony Modungwo	24
Vicki Acquah	26
Prince Ken Osei	31
Wilson 'thePoet' Amooro	33
Tribhawan Kaul	35
Terika McQuinn	37
Sujan Bhsattacharyya	39
Satwik Mishra	40
Shareef Abdur-Rasheed	41
Elizabeth Esguerra Castillo	44

Table of Contents ... *continued*

Quest Purple	45
Drezhon Arquis Holloway	47
Alan W. Jankowski	48
Fiyinfoluwa Onarinde	49
Shihi Venus	51
Lady Elegance	52
Rosemarie Howard	53
Jamie Bond	55
Diane Sismour	62
Robert Gibbons	65
June Barefield	71
hülya n yılmaz	75
Janet P. Caldwell	77
William S. Peters, Sr.	80

Epilogue — 87

Madiba Biography	89
Quotes of Madiba	101
The Gallery	104

Madiba

Nelson Rolihlahla Mandela

July 18, 1918 ~ December 5, 2013

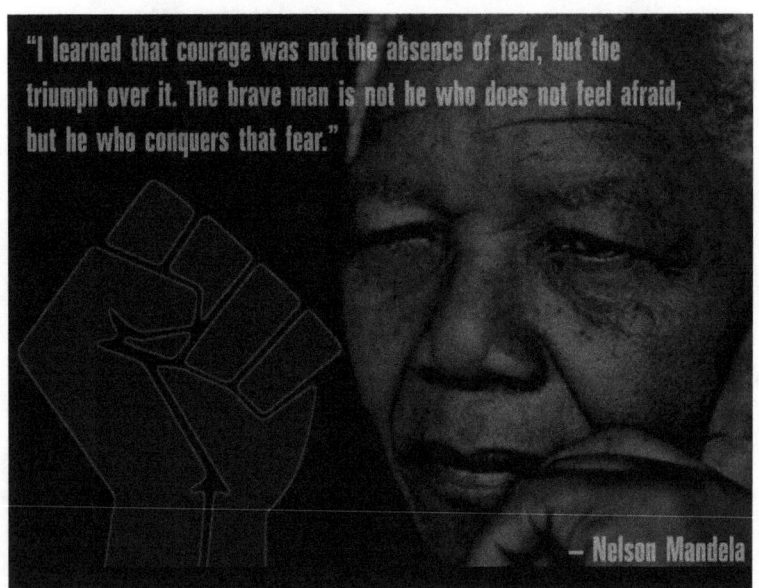

INVICTUS

Out of the night that covers me,
Black as the Pit from pole to pole,
I thank whatever gods may be
For my unconquerable soul.

In the fell clutch of circumstance
I have not winced nor cried aloud.
Under the bludgeonings of chance
My head is bloody, but unbowed.

Beyond this place of wrath and tears
Looms but the Horror of the shade,
And yet the menace of the years
Finds, and shall find, me unafraid.

It matters not how strait the gate,
How charged with punishments the scroll.
I am the master of my fate:
I am the captain of my soul.

William Ernest Henley

There is no passion to be found playing small - in settling for a life that is less than the one you are capable of living.

~ **Nelson Mandela**

Mandela

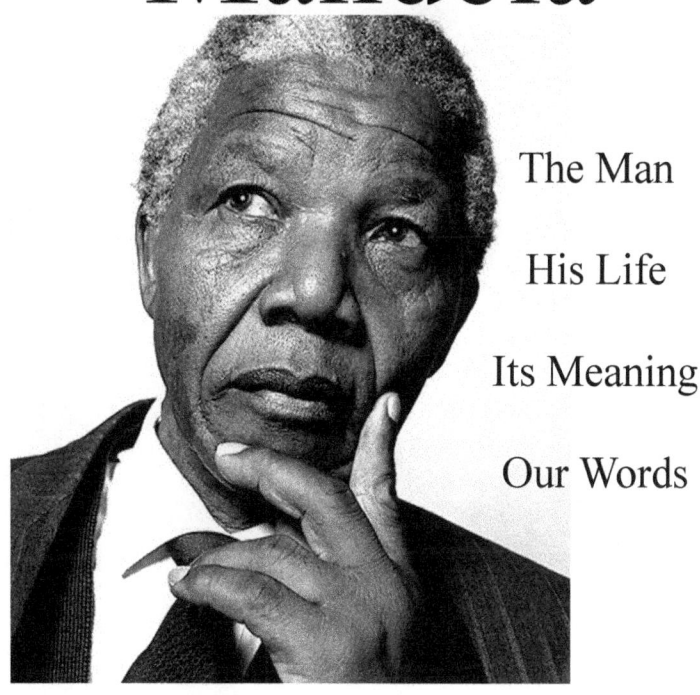

The Man

His Life

Its Meaning

Our Words

Poetry . . . Commentary & Stories
The Anthological Writers

inner child press, ltd.

Nelson Mandela

This World has seen some remarkable human beings who have left a mark. Martin Luther King, Gandhi, John Lennon were assassinated early in their lives.

Nelson Mandela is the exception, he spent 27 years in prison, of his long life a century long, he came from South African royalty, studied law at the university, a brilliant person, who was able to combat colonialism and institutionalized racism breaking the monstrous jaws of apartheid, against incredible odds he succeeded in establishing multiracial elections, he was elected president of South Africa, combating poverty, he championed for human rights, established health care.

Mandela has received international acclaim, Nobel peace prize, Order of Lenin, US presidential medal of freedom, amongst hundreds of international awards.
Such an exceptional human being hardly ever has come to Earth to bless us all, such potential has never been realized to such an extent in the World, planet Earth.

Only recently the president of the USA, the eloquently spoken but his promises broken Obama, visited South Africa, as Mandela the father of the nation was in his death bed. Affirmative we must be and call upon a transmutation of a great proportion, Mandela to pass into Obama in spirit, this will make a major difference, hoping for such a miracle to take place whereby Obama returns to America with Mandela's spirit inside his chest, let us pray for a miracle to take place; when at this point in time we need to see truthfulness override political jargon.

Mandela

Will the president of the U.S.A stand up and be a great World leader like Mandela? He is in a position to make the difference, to deliver us from pending disaster.

Such be the affirmation, let there be light, let Mandela's legacy shine bright and become as such the guiding light all nations can embrace with delight.

Vensan Kamberk

Mandela

Homage To Ascending Master Mandela

Nelson Mandela is an awesome man.
He stood up for us when there was a ban.
He went to jail for the sins of others,
and got together with a group of brothers.

Nelson Mandela was born in the village of Umtatu,
They had no idea what that little baby would do.
The first name he was given was Rolihlahla,
He was given a few names was Nelson Mandela.
Madiba was the name that he loved the best,
It was one that he held closest to his chest.

Nelson's great-grandfather ruled the Thembu tribe,
They were noble people and had much pride.
His early life was full of much 'custom, ritual and taboo',
Most of this happened in the village of Qunu.

Nelson's father died when he was around nine,
Reflecting on this now, it was an auspicious sign.
Nelsons mother was not wealthy, did not have a penny,
so thinking about his future, took him to Palace Mqhekezweni.
Jongintaba and his wife Noengland raised him as their own
with their children Justice and Nomafu till they were grown.

Although neither of his parents could read or write,
This would never stop Madiba from vision to fight.
He went to University and studied English, politics and law
If only the ones who were teaching him could have forsaw,
What this young man would do to the country he loved
He would turn it around, he'd not see his people shoved.
Nelson made friends with people from Sotu
It was also here he met Oliver Tambo.
Madiba had many more talents you know,

Mandela

He knew much about gardening and all that does grow
Nelson loved to dance and play sport,
He was outstanding on any sort of court.

Nelson Mandela is an awesome man.
He stood up for us when there was a ban.
He went to jail for the sins of others
and got together with a group of brothers.

While Justice and Nelson were doing their degrees,
They visited home to share their expertise.
The family had arranged marriages in store for them,
Jo'burg was the different idea, from them, did stem.

He stayed with his cousin and met Walter Sisulu,
During this friendship, alot they would go through.
Madiba was the only native African student at university,
An excellent example of the South African lack of diversity.

By '44 commenced his path with the ANC,
He wanted his countryman to be totally free,
To decide their fate without the control of others,
So he banded together with like minded brothers.

By '48 apartheid grew stronger and stronger,
but Nelson could not put up with it any longer.
He rallied his brothers for boycotts and strikes,
He encouraged his countrymen to get on their bikes.

He served the white man up his shame.
He showed them it was not game,
To take away another mans freedom,
Just because you want to steal their Kingdom.

Mandela

At first Nelson did not want a racially united front,
He wanted it for Africans, lets be really blunt.
However, he did change his mind over this stance,
Now South African stood a hopeful chance.

Nelson admired Ghandi's stance of non-violence
It seemed like the road of the least resistance.
By '53 the ANC had 100,000 supporters
They started to attract journalists and reporters.

Arrested for breaking the Suppression of Communist Act,
They picked on him because he wasn't of vanilla extract.
So Mandela and Tambo opened their own law firm,
They wanted to see their oppressors squirm like a worm.

Police banned Mandela from making public appearances,
but he wasn't to bothered, and often took his chances.
His marriage to Evelyn sadly ended in divorce,
It had been difficult, but had now had run its course.

A social worker called Winnie got his attention,
Winnie was a patriot too did I mention
They married in Bizana in '58
Less that a year from his divorce, it must have been fate.

The government put Madiba on trial in '58,
They wanted him locked away, did the state
They accused him of treason, for his loyalty to his land,
Madiba didn't care one bit, he'd make a stand.
By '61 he had been found not guilty,
They were not happy, they had no pity.

Nelson Mandela is an awesome man.
He stood up for us when there was a ban.
He went to jail for the sins of others
and got together with a group of brothers.

Mandela

The government of the time banned the ANC,
They had had enough of the political detainee.
So Nelson partitioned for a military wing,
He took it one step further than Martin Luther King.

The go ahead for the Umkhonto we Sizwe was given,
Now they ANC would be militarily driven.
Mandela was arrested in '62
Much hard labour he had to do.

In '63 the main leaders of the ANC were arrested,
They understood this was a time they were tested.
Overthrowing the state by violence was not allowed,
So they said, those that were unbowed.

Nelson Mandela is an awesome man.
He stood up for us when there was a ban.
He went to jail for the sins of others
and got together with a group of brothers.

As he took the stand, he made a speech
It really was awesome, quite a peach,
He expressed the hopes and fears of his nation.
It was heard by the world, this compelling narration.

In '64 himself and his comrades were sentenced to life,
It was sad for Madiba, to say goodbye to his wife.
From '62-84 Robben Island Prison held our hero,
Then Pollsmoor had him, till the countdown was zero.

He went to jail for twenty seven years,
Those that loved him cried many tears.
We went on marches to free his soul,
We wanted him out, that was our goal.

Mandela

While in prison Nelson's reputation grew and grew,
It didn't seem to matter what de Klerk put him through.
He would not negotiate his release under any terms,
If it meant compromising, he'd just watch them squirm.

Our superhero was released in 1990 to jubilation,
The world had been waiting for this one celebration.
The ANC gave him the leading role of their organisation,
He got to work fast, not one for procrastination.

Our Madiba was made President of his country at last.
He was honoured for his struggle, he was man of class.
He helped with AIDS, football and peace in Africa
but he wanted to retire and get back to botanica.

After he was given the Nobel Peace Prize for his work
For taking on and ridding South Africa of de Klerk,
He retired from the world of the camera and light
He had done his bit, now it was another's fight.

Nelson stands for alot you see.
He cared about us and wanted us free
To love each other as equals its true
He stood up for people like me and you.
Now he is sick and we send our love
He appeared to us like a beautiful dove
He wanted no more than justice and peace
His work was quite the conversation piece.
Get well soon Ascended Master Mandela
You brought South Africa under one umbrella.

Deryn de Temple

Mandela

Madiba Lives

He healed humanity
By submitting self to be afflicted by inhumanity
He defeated defeat
By strangling fear to death
Madiba uprooted the weeds of apartheid
With the hoe of selflessness.

He is an oak of great height
He paid the price for greatness
By standing on a quicksand
He held on
Until a rock appeared beneath.

He walked in perilous ways
A long walk, he called it
A walk through the land of captivity
He was sustained during the journey
Faith, determination and courage
Accompanied him during the walk
He came out freed
Not alone but with all.

He bailed freedom out of jail
By living with freedom in jail
Both came out together victorious
Live Madiba, freedom still lives
Hold the hands of freedom
Raise your fist; a sledge hammer
And let death flee
Knowing you still yearn for freedom.

Kolade Olanrewaju Freedom

Freedom Is Not Free; Madiba Paid The Price

It aches my heart to read the comment of a fellow who accused Mandela of selling out his people by continuing the white agenda when he became the first black president of South Africa in order to gain recognition, fame and acceptability. What a demeaning comment!

Nelson Mandela acted as Moses for the South Africans and you can't justly accuse him for the woes that befell the nation thereafter. Moses helped free his people from the Egyptians but that does not mean he could be accused of the woes that befell the Israelites after being freed from captivity. Freedom is the greatest gift one can offer another. Being jailed for 27 years so as to eradicate apartheid is enough to overshadow any flaws you might relate to Mandela.

With freedom comes great responsibility. He fought for freedom because he believed man should have a mind of his own and also be allowed to freely pursue his cause."A man can free another from physical captivity but not mental captivity"...

Madiba freed his people physically but mental freedom can only be gained internally. The condition of blacks in South Africa might not be pleasing, but never blame Madiba. He offered freedom, destroyed inequality, restored dignity and peace to the nation. What more do you want from him?...His life? You are about to have that. He is suffering today because of humanity, 27 years in jail with labor is enough to deteriorate one's health.

Mandela

Mandela dehumanized inhumanity to humanize humanity. He fought against white dominance likewise black dominance. Honor him not defame him....If only you could spend a day in Jail for a brother, you will know what sacrifice is and adore those who have been slaughtered indirectly for others to live a "meaningful life" Don't you believe it is better to die free than to live in captivity. Don't you believe it is better to live poor than to be rich in captivity.

Disagreeing with me makes me remember the Israelites who blamed God for bringing them out of captivity to suffer....

No matter how you defame my father (Nelson Mandela);you still cannot
disassociate his name from FREEDOM.

A costly price he paid
A costly honour he earned.

Kolade Olanrewaju Freedom

Mandela

In a South African hospital lies a man

No not just a man, a symbol of freedom

Of determination, of justice and peace

His name is Nelson Mandela

The heartbeat of a country

The soul of his people

A symbol of persistence

A hammer of resistance

Imprisoned for most of his life

Apartheid's worst enemy

His faith would not falter

His strength would not wane

He is the lifeblood of the people

The leader of the new day

A king who has regained his throne

Yet humble and quiet

He comes now to the end

Mandela

Dignity still radiates from his soul

He prepares for his homecoming

To walk along the glory road

Martin, Malcolm, and Gandhi

Stand and await him

He will be welcomed

He will be at home.

uthi, Makwandiswe kuni inceba noxolo nothando

Mercy unto you, and peace, and love, be multiplied

These things I wish upon you

Nelson Rolihlahla Mandela

In honor of Mr. Mandela, who transitioned to the land of the ancestors at the age of 95

Anthony Arnold

Celebration (for Nelson Mandela)

His earthly body is gone

But his spirit abounds

His walk is done

But the journey remains

Our sorrow is large

But the joy is immense

We have lost only a man

But gained an ancestor

He would not want us to cry

But raise our voices in joy

Bless him as he transitions

Forever hold his name in our hearts

So shout it from the highest mountain

To be heard in the valley low

Let his name be heard

Mandela…Mandela…Mandela!

Mandela

Uthi, Makwandiswe kuni inceba noxolo nothando

Mercy unto you, and peace, and love, be multiplied

These things I wish upon you

Nelson Rolihlahla Mandela

Anthony Arnold

Mr. Mandela

Normally one would sit confounded,

when confronted by a nation weeping.

The force of emotions screamed forth as one voice.

The flood of tears as a legend passes into forever.

Not for this man however.

For when this man died,

a world of man woman and child, cried...

We weep for the loss of a peace maker.

We weep for the loss of a teacher.

We weep for the loss of a real leader.

For every tear,

weeped by every soul on this planet,

you will be held on high.

You were a great man, Sir Mandela.

You lay a foundation solid enough to support the weight of

a world of us who are to follow deep within your footsteps.

You laid this foundation solid in a beautiful continent to

serve as an example to the rest of the world to follow.

Us who sat in your shadow and learned from the best are

ready to take up where you left off.

For the example you set, the world owes you a great debt of

gratitude.

Mandela

And we who have a voice to be heard, make you this promise...

We will be heard...

You taught us well...

It is now our job to take, as the teacher, and SPEAK TO BE HEARD!!

We will be heard.

We will make you proud Sir Mandela, for you made us proud.

Rest now assured, that we KNOW the might of the pen versus the sword.

Rest in peace and assurance, that we learned well.

Goodnight sweet sir... rest well.. you earned it..

Intricate B aka Jason Brierly

THE HUT

Way back, when the sky kissed the land, in the tender rolling hills of Mvezo, sits a little simple thatched mud hut. From within the circular walls of this little hut, in this gentle place, at the feet of the whispering Mbashe River, the birthing voice of Mama Nosekeni Nkedama sang out to hills and the birth of her son Rolihlahla echoed through the ancient land, rejoicing his arrival. The hut smiled quietly, proud in the sun.

Rolihlahla, "Pulling-the branch-from the –tree", Troublesome, call him what you may, but he had arrived that bright African day, with a steely determination and his future determined by the stars, to change the course of his country's history. The hut knew as soon as the child was born, that he was special.

Time marched into the future, events occurred, terrible events and Rolihlahla marched with it, fist raised. The hut just watched from its gentle hills, impotent and sad at seeing what was happening. Time passed, everything aged, white head, cracked walls, loves loved, births birthed, adobe renewed, politics in upheaval, thatch crumbling, man imprisoned, weeds rife. The world spun, the hut's man did

Mandela

great things, was removed by inane injustice and returned with a vengeance, dignity and love without malice, while the hut sat in her gentle hills.

The great man grew old and left this world, for a more compassionate place. He left the world's people weeping with their sad missing. The little hut still sat, rain-dropped tears dripping down her crumbling walls, but proud she was there at his beginning, that she had watched him grow and now she welcomed him home with open arms, "Welcome home my son". When his body was safe within the embrace of those gentle hills and his soul had flown to heaven on the wings of Angels, the hut breathed a sigh of relief, within the winds of Thembuland and finally released her vigilance.

SUE LOBO 2013

Rolihlahla : Mandela

A little Picinnini born in be-hutted place of thorn, dust & lowly goat,
Not knowing that one day he'd fight for his people to have the vote,
Born Xhosa, of noble birth & from the proud, brave & ancient tribe,
To us Nelson Mandela, but Rolihlahla his true & real name inscribed.

Known & hunted, the biggest terrorist within his sad but beautiful land,
Living & fighting by the laws of those white men, so long ago planned,
Put on trial, found guilty, so very wrongly castigated & in the end jailed,
While the people of his struggling country prayed & sadly cried & wailed.

Caged on Robben Island, that very isolated & old Isle of lost ancient lepers,
Incarcerated, Manacled in iron-chained & tight white man's sorry fetters,
Where behind iron bars, lonely years flew fast & apologizing, past you by,
And you Rolihlahla, the world's errant hero, would sit quietly & silently cry.

The long awaited day arrived, when Mandela at last walked proud & free,
And his life-long struggle scribbled in the African dust, became lost history,
Washed away in time, from our forgetful memories by drops of falling rain,
Leaving behind only the scribblings of the world's receding & shameful pain.

Mandela

Mandela, our dear Madiba of all world's lands & of millennium's many moons,
We hear your voice & your wisdom, whispered within the ancient tribal tunes,
Our mentor of humanity, we now ask, what goes through your heavenly mind?
Looking down upon your African land, do you now ask, "What have I left behind?"

SUE LOBO

Mandela

Destiny . . . a Tribute

It has been almost a hundred years since a special child was born in South Africa
A child, a very special child, that would grow up to surpass, most men we would ever know
A man that would do whatever it would take for his people of South Africa
Never thinking of himself, standing up for the people whether it be friend or foe.

Growing up from nothing, but the people were always on his mind
Sanct...ifying for all with no questions ever asked, no sacrifice ever too big
This man was always smiling and kind
Using peace and democracy, a solution to any problem he would try and find.

Giving of himself like no there man that I know
Twenty-seven years of his life in prison, in a cage, he was confined
But even after all this time, when released, he blamed no one, peace on his side, he had no foes
From prison to the first black president of his country, from the people and his country he never declined.

Peace radiated from his smile, the smile was contagious, just like the shining sun
With his infectious ways, he brought an entire country to freedom
With respect and gratitude, he became the father of his nation, from this he would never run
All the people of his country, they were his children, for them he would pay any sum.

Mandela

If only there were more like this man of peace, this man using kindness as his weapon
But people like this are few and far between, and there is something very special about them
Seems they were born to be a leader or lead, now he is gone, but the hearts he made a mark upon
His ideology on the horizon, his ideas his very soul always bright and never dim.

Now at ninety-five, he has left us hopefully he is now in a better place
In a place, just like he wanted this old world to some day be
No more shall we witness the radiation just like the sun that came from his face
All of us should take a lesson from Nelson Mandela, his destiny was surely meant to be.

Lanaia Lee

Mandela

The Sheraton Lobby : Ann Arbor, Michigan

It is overwhelmed

with Christmas music

and I've no grounds

on which to argue.

It is less than three weeks

until the twenty-fifth.

Hotel guests absently hum

along with the carols

on their way in

and out of breakfast.

One woman,

watching television

by the front desk

weeps.

Complimentary newspapers

are folded and stacked

on a table near the entrance,

announcing that Mandela

is no more.

Steve Brightman

MANDELA

A man jailed for 27 years
But later became president
A bulwark against apartheid,
Corrupting forces of anarchy
And decay; aided by the
Pure fire of discipline
A man who preferred prison
Than imprisoned conscience
A man with a large heart
And inconceivable capacity
A man seasoned by reality
And fortified by long
Experience of men and affairs
A man who can quell riots
With only lightning-dressed
Words instead of live bullets
A man whose achievements
Didn't seep into the lining of
His heart rather idolization of
His excellence challenged him
To greater accomplishments

Mandela

The soul of discretion and a
Veritable engine of good works
In Africa, in our Africa where
Many societal shepherds with
Whitewashed character have led
Their sheep astray Mandela like
The good shepherd laid down his
Life for his sheep binding his
Together with cords of discipline
Rolling heavy black cloud from
The spirit of South Africa
Mandela you're my measure of
All a man should be.
A legend has taken his exit
To God be the Glory.

Anthony Modungwo

Mandela

Take Your Rest

Oh pale moon what
does dull your glimmer-glow.?

Oh dreary sun-why
hide your face behind
dark clouds -?

Common is thy light that shines.
What good is it for you to shine
when good has -left here
when the good has left us here.?

Today when saint's are
no longer sinners.

We search hearts
and cannot find even
one, to measure up
in these perilous times.

We cannot see,
In these dark days.
Considering in all the universe

He is my favorite person
Dead or alive-
I will stand by what he stood for-

I may be welling up tears,
and do not tell me not to cry

I am not as nice
I am not as patient.
I am not as kind.
I will tap-dance on your liver

Mandela

and stuff your hateful words
towards your tonsils,
until you choke on them.
No maneuverings-can save you.

He will wear his boxing Gloves.
STILL MY champion in another
space...Madba is now my
secret weapon-

Spirit lighter than a feather,
Unburdened...One true
"Heavy Weight."

His discipline made me his disciple.
His name can crack all my codes

He is my secret question, my password
that opens revelations.

I have seen thousand's of years pass,
And thousands more will come and go

Just like Jesus's story -
distorted-with truth convoluted.

We must not let them
add nor take away
although they will try.

We will be watchful,
like international rederic spies.

Mandela

The cowards are coming out;
In route-

Getting ready to get their dibs in
and sucker punching his name.

But Nelson has his boxing gloves on
On another plane.

I will trap them in their lies
I will send them to where
there flesh will be cursed.

We have to protect him
from Gossip and blame.

Hold up the banner-
He shall be sanctified
In his new Land

We know him as a man.
A hue-man A true man.

Forward ever Backward never...
I will wait until I see the
light in the eyes of the sufferers,
before I smile again while on earth.

See this is what
I witnessed in my own life-time.

If any imbecile dare to utter
a mumbling word against his anointing,
I will draw on every resource,
collect every debt owed me.

Mandela

Sacrifices he gave were
for gains to be made.
He who willingly for
us "spent" his life?

By example he led-not much on talk
Observations and notations,
As he took that long walk.

Oh pale moon what
does dull your glimmer glow.?

Oh dreary sun-why
hide your face behind
dark clouds ?
What good is thy light-
that shines.?

What good is left here?
When the good has
left us here, today.
When saint's are
no longer sane.

Do not be disturbed Nelson
We search hearts.
and cannot find even one,
Who can measure up in
these perilous times. ..

Did the time
committed no crime.
You were no sell out-
Because sell out's "get out."

Mandela

He has now gone and left..!
Has done his ultimate Best.

Now Nelson,-MaDeba...
Until we meet again
be Comfortable in the arms of the
one who loved, us enough
to make you..

And Loved you enough to take you.
Allow your soul to rest.
For you have done your best...
For you have done your best

Vicki Acquah

Mandela

an ode to MADIBA

Unto the pantheon of the all-time greats

Shall humanity pray you

As fervent appraisals flood in

From the city-centres of all ages, creeds and dispensations

To the South-west townships of your rainbow nation

We salute you,

And even if the earth doesn't hear us,

the heavens will

And in no day shall we trespass

On your indelibly marked oratorical seriousness

 At Half Staff

Indeed, "no man is born hating"

So we'll keep your unsurpassed memory in blossoming

spectacles

And allow its radiance

To cast light on our fits and starts

Although, "a long walk to freedom has it been"

At the Isthmus of Panama

Mandela

Shall we revere your sense of humour
As we seize not
To regale our tittle-tattle
With songs of obeisance

Indeed, it's true that whenever a finger
dips in palm oil, it soils the entire hand
And if the yam used in sacrifice doesn't
die prematurely, it'll eventually germinate
So, may your remains descend to its eternal abode
As we eulogize and salve consciences with
your exemplary lead
Just like a diamond, you'll always be almost flawless
Fare thee well...
Tata Madiba !

Prince Ken Osei

Mandela

Prisoner to President: Nelson Mandela

A tender heart is one that willingly forgives
With all the right reasons
To pay back, love showered instead.
Concentrating not on the scars, counting the stars
Of hope, blind to mortal eyes.

Learning early in life that:
Revenge is heavier to carry than love.
A long, long walk
Sometimes so wearied to talk
The only energy that may be left
Is to hold the reasons of the seasons bold.

Twenty-seven years of toil
His spirit was broken
But his love for humanity wasn't taken

From a prisoner to a President
Hardwork wasn't enough
Passion was burnt.

Mandela

From zero to hero

He showed us we can rise

From nothing to something

[Even if we don't inherit, special genes]

we should nev'r forget to commit our all to it.

Wilson 'thePoet' Amooro

Mandela

Madiba, an angel of peace

The Sun sets always to herald a new dawn
A dove freed from cage, flew relentlessly
Setting those perceptions right, gone awfully wrong
After 27 years of quarantine
Oh, the dove is now no more.
Long live Madiba, an angel of peace.

Set free from silence with unbroken spirit
Metamorphosing into human strength
Wielding courage
To challenge brute force and injustice
Oh, the dove is now no more.
Long live Madiba, an angel of peace.

Sufferings in privation
Taking bull by its own horns
Symbol of people's struggle and aspirations
Lighting candle of peace, love and compassion
Oh, the dove is now no more.
Long live Madiba, an angel of peace.

Mandela

Those limestone shine on your calloused hands
Shaping the castle of hope for millions
To build a society sans raciest and discriminatory thoughts
Shepherded the flock to ultimate freedom
Oh, the dove is now no more.
Long live Madiba, an angel of peace.

Basking in sunshine, rainbow nation rejoice
Absorbing rays to burn thoughts of the dark
Emerging multi culturalism raising hopes
Inspiring life, a lesson written in golden ink
Oh, the dove is now no more.
Long live Madiba, an angel of peace.

Pray your soul be always at peace
Yet it is not the end
The world owes to your masterly investment skills
Let the world pay you back now the rich dividend
Oh, the dove is now no more.
Long live Madiba, an angel of peace.

Tribhawan Kaul

Mandela

"Let Freedom Ring"

Dear African brothas and sistahs
Did you hear my voice of freedom
long before they let me out
from behind those jail cells bars,
where I spent twenty-seven long years?
It was there
I learned from my own experience,
praying day and night through my pain
hoping that emotional scars of yesterday will not stay!
Children know in your hearts that you are somebody special,
Rise up like the sun!
grow from the strong roots of our
ancestors reminiscing on their sacrifice harvest the
fruitful seeds of perseverance and pride,
Martin's dream...
Thank-you Lord Jesus Martin dream has not died!
Listen wit your ears it's still breathing fresh air!
I swear ! The dream is alive
There is a heartbeat and a pulse,
As a people we can't afford to go faint,
I'm not a saint I do stand for something,
I'm strong
I'm tired of falling for anything!
Don't you know baby,
I am your father
I will bend over forward and backward for you,
climb all those Congo hills and dark valleys too!
In a few,
reality will show up,
delivery some heavy doses!
I already told you how it was gonna be!

Mandela

Read my all my letters to my beloved grand-daughter,
and the rest of my family back in Johannesburg!
Right now, I'm in heaven floating on the highest white cloud,
let my letters tell of the real love I had for each one of you,
til we meet again,
let them hold you! Don't cry for me,
remember the kind of man I truly was,
I lived I didn't exist just because.
I exercised humility for others!
I never mined carrying their heavy weight on my shoulders!
I over stand
My time was well-served
I never really got the full- respect from my counterparts !
I deserve I wore the badge of honor,
I am ultimate leader,
My job was to lift them up!
The bells of freedom & equality are ringing!
My children are playing holding hands,
making bright promise future plans
dancing and singing songs of oneness,in unison,
One by one,
I shall speak the words upon my tongue,
open thy lips blurt out !
Loudly, I didn't always shine,
my work reflected bright beams of light!
My grave stone scribes,
Mandela my name I left my mark on this whorl,
My last will in testament states let freedom ring!
As you bow your heads, say a prayer for me!
allows my lessons to resonate deep within. Amen!

Poetess, Terika McQuinn

Mandela

Still is Nelson...

Rose up, as he, upto the sky,

Still the feet far down the soil;

Droplets of sweat make the being

Through the lanes of ceaseless toil.

Who cares for, where stops life

In the texture of well-built sects,

All the fables creep to a silence,

Towering guards are at the walls, erect.

Then comes he, down the shore,

The whirlwind touches the hills,

Rocky curves know the deepest thirst;

And him, the womb surely feels.

The meadows and also the cattle-boys,

The springing rivers and the sailors upon,

Torn out huts and wrecking faces inside –

All they know, now, there comes he – the Nelson.

And as he passes, there still remains he;

The faith of millions gives him the birth,

Everyday, in the touch of a peeping sun,

Resurrects him here, in the myriad worth.

Sujan Bhsattacharyya

The way you did it 'Mandela'

No one could again inspire the sphere,

The way you did it 'Mandela'

A savior,

In the darkest thought.

A revolutionary,

Without any turbulent shout.

The world of hope,

Which you had brought.

Fighting with the patience,

Against the draught.

We overlook the lesson,

Which you had taught.

Even God needed your presence,

That's why you have been caught.

But,

No one could again prompt the world,

The way you did it 'Mandela'

Satwik Mishra

Mandela

Amanda Madiba!

some are called for certain
test
blessed with what stands out
from the rest!
touched, blessed!
tasks heaped on
that few men think on,
speak on,
much less act upon

Madiba, Madiba, Rolihlahla, Mandela,
Rolihlahla, Xhosa for "Trouble-Maker"
Xhosa son born from Royal line
chosen one!
lead takers time!

Amanda! Amanda! Amanda!
(Freedom! Freedom! Freedom!)

was the cry!

Let my people go!
we won't take it no more
Apartheid must die
even if we as well
better then existing
in this hell!

to try and die is worth the
try
think of the story
they will tell!

Mandela

Madiba was the one upon
whom the task fell!

and soon was heard the
freedom bell!

Amanda! Amanda! Amanda!

amazing cry burning in the
belly of the beast
raised to a boil
heard round the world
north, south, west, east,

Amanda! Amanda! Amanda!

amazing cry, as worlds leaders
knew and stood by
watched many, many die
as we learn,
more concerned about
the gold they buy!
willing to be in bed with
living a lie was nothing new
this is what they do
what their used to!
Soweto, the mines, Joburg,
have you heard
young lions
wanted to live but prepared
for dying!
rather then exist
to make apartheid cease and
desist was worth trying!
overcome fear!

Mandela

and Madiba, Rolihlahla was put
away for 27 years!

until the day was to be when
Madiba walked free into the arms
of Winnie and a sea of humanity!

quite a journey for a man who was
picked to pick up the relay stick
and run, carry a nation into the sun
almost 95 years from the day he
appeared and yet even today
no matter what they say

apartheid is still not done!
reflect on the ripple effect
the work of Rolihlahla,
the "TroubleMaker"
has just begun!

says da beat of the African Drum!

Amanda! Amanda! Amanda!

(Dedicated to Nelson Mandela, the Winnie's and Steven Biko's and the many whose names we don't know)

Shareef Abdur-Rasheed

A Man Named Madiba

It is in unity that we can change the world
No separation of beliefs and no color differences,
Here was a man who trampled the gruesome impact of discrimination
Inspired by his powerful words,
He bridged the gap of misunderstandings among nations
No black, yellow, white or brown
We are all one with an ultimate vision against disparity.
Madiba, you are one true hero not just in the eyes of your African descent,
But as well as in the hearts of men all over the world
Who were living witnesses of your humane integrity and love for peace,
Your name and outstanding legacy will live on for generations upon generations to come
They will honor the great endeavors you bestowed upon your fellowmen
Madiba, Africa must be proud to have you as his Son,
May the world not forget one great man like you.

Elizabeth Esguerra Castillo

Mandela Mandala

Mandela dreamt, his dream fulfilled

27 years of imprisonment, his will unbent

A myriad lifetimes in apartheid, our ambassador spent

His purpose, he met…his freedom he would get

So, finally he succumbed to death

But, not in vain, was his legacy

It was never wasted, like his humanity

You did not lose the race, Mandela, you are now beyond

You passed the torch to us with the social baton

Humanitarianism, the next leg of the marathon, will be for those who are now alive…living

A poet's words are immortal, a sacrifice worth giving

The Mandela mandala, stand up, reach out, simply outstanding

Yet, words you spoke, still valiantly exist

To our mother, Winnie, we soul embrace, with a kiss

Mandela

From all in the hearts, whose eyes are moist with a tearful mist

Rain poured out with a storm, unrehearsed

Like the tears we shed for you, the first…Mandiba

Your children will tell your tale…You are an iconic social legend!

Death is not the end of your mission, it is only the beginning!

Quest Purple

Mandela

My name is Drezhon Arquis Holloway and I am 9 years old and I like poetry. I am like

Mandela because we had a movie at school about him and my teacher wanted us to know how

good that man was. I love him 1,000 percent because my Mommy told me that he was a great

man and he did great things in Africa. I know he was very old when he died, so he could be

my play Grandfather. Now he is gone and I feel sad because he was a really important world

leader, like Martin Luther King was and he is gone, too. I know I am just a little kid, but kids

have to look up to their elders. I am like Mandela because my mommy loves Mandela and my

mommy loves me! My mommy said, "Out of the mouth of babes…" but I am not a baby!

Drezhon Arquis Holloway

Mandela

Madiba

He was the voice of those who had no voice,
The spokesman for the oppressed.
He became a true hero to the downtrodden,
Who had been denied their basic human rights.
There were those who tried to stop him,
But he proved himself a true force of nature.
Because you can arrest the man,
But you can't arrest his vision.
And while they could lock him in a cell,
They could not lock away his ideas.
And while they could put shackles on his body,
They could not put shackles on his dreams.
And those dreams live on,
To the very ends of the Earth,
In every classroom where black and white
Learn side by side.
In every place of worship,
Where young and old gather together,
In every peaceful demonstration,
Where tyranny falls, and liberty reigns triumphant.
And in the cry of every newborn,
That they be born into a world of hope and tolerance,
Where equality and civil rights are the norm.
For you can bury the man, but not his beliefs.
And though his voice may be silent,
His spirit will live on and on.

Alan W. Jankowski

Mandela

Rohilala

The sorcerer of words in another world

Stares into his magical prism,

In his prism sprouts the hourglass

The hourglass speaks of the time and of the man

In whose ashes a voracious flame burns for the world.

Every night when the chi of the prism guides him through her gates

He finds multiple shades of love in a flawed being.

In this man he discovers the humanity of man.

The sorcerer finds a man who carries his world on his shoulders

And his words he carries in his hearth.

In the prism he met the porter of all troubles

Who forgives the hunter of the hunted.

In his land he made new laws love

Unlike his brothers who versioned new acronyms of death.

In an the envelope called the porter's hearth

The sorcerer found freedom and love.

Fiyinfoluwa Onarinde

Mandela ~ Father Of The Nation

I smile in reigning honor to know of you

I get excited to know you're another

Legend in my historical lifetime...

You have given my generation past

Present and future so much to be added

To life history of the Father Legends

From the Civil Rights Era

The Struggles you endured, the strength

Of Job while imprisoned your strength

To take on the Truth to be told by killing The lies that has been locked in cold Hearted authoritative figures your Nobel Peace Prize, Bhsrat Ratna 1990,

Order of Lenin, and Presidential Medal

Of Freedom has given me dignity, stature, diligence, pride to give , mental strength and a peacefulness of

Non Violence deep in my heart

You've given us courage, because of

Your courageousness, continuing on

Mandela

My donations of giving of my time

Through it all you still displayed your

Smile...what hides behind that face

Where does your mind find a peaceful

Place...

You ate too huge in character in name

Everything you've done so ...Im going to salute you in Stevie Wonder's song-

I JUST CALLED TO SAY I LOVE YOU

Thank you...Father Of The Nation

Nelson Rolihlahla Mandela (Madida)

7-18-1918 * 12-5-13

Qunu, Eastern Cape

Shihi Venus

Nelson Mandela

We mourn the loss of a great man, Nelson Mandela
95 candles burned representing the light of each year
His footprints grazed and walked the lands for he was and
Always will be a beloved icon of our people.
Nelson Mandela not only transformed South Africa and
Defeated apartheid, he opened our eyes to his principles
Freedom for all, we became believers he showed us what it
Meant to fight for freedom, to be educated and informed
To raise our fist to the sky and resist societies so called reform
Nelson Mandela's spirit shall forever reign in our hearts
Just like the tears that flow like the Nile bursting into streams
For his soul has departed the earth, but the struggle and fight
Will continue until there is equality and freedom for all people

LadyElegance 2014

"To deny people their human rights, is to challenge their very humanity"

Nelson Mandela

Madiba ~ Mandela

King of Kings
fought for rights for all
not just one
sacraficed flesh and mentality
for governmental principalities
Segregation remained and
prayer stayed always the same
A man with a conscious of
what is right and what is wrong
still those in political office tried
to keep the same song
A Poet of Poet's
instrumental in Freedom for a nation
who cried
lashes and bashes
Archbishop TUTU walked and walked
with a society shouts of
release him to the sunlight
allow us to touch HIM
27--27--27(Screaming) years
his humbleness
his vision
his patience
his word's
through the land of anger
human kindness and generosity
at a standstill, whispering
hatred later visual via a
verbally kill
Apartheid at it's
best,

Mandela

Glory to God it now
lays to rest because of a MAN
dignified at HIS best
His soft spoken voice never raised
the punisher always amazed
of HIS demeanor never crazed but
spiritually sounded of Forgiveness
of those sinfully grounded
Wisdom surrounds them
people want to be like HIM
South Africa dance dance
like you have never danced
before,scream and shout
Kindness and genuine
a Man of integrity
a Man of Peace
A Man of Courage
A Healer
A Mentor
A Icon
A Noble Peace Prize Winner
A Man of History
Dance---Dance---Dance
Mandela
Mandela
Mandela
forever We will Shout HIS NAME......

Rosemarie Howard

Mandela

Lese Majesty

Dear Nelson Mandela,

I have waited to hear what they were going to do with you and as I suspected; they have made the decision to pull the plug..... Just know that I was praying for you way before you got sick... You Sir; were a powerful symbol of resistance to the anti-apartheid movement and your outstanding purpose is magnified as a heritage that will never be forgotten, nor will the imprint of your movement fade from our hearts and souls...

Rest assured that we have publicly joined the throng while fiercely applauding you and your purpose driven strides so when you said: The Struggle is My Life ... Oh WE thoroughly overstand that statement and I for one am not worried about Gods favor for you because I know that for many years now you have bravely stated that I am prepared to die.....

Unfortunately; we have gone from civil rights to uncivil rights... Where although the issues of segregation have gotten better it somehow cascaded into worse conditions...

Our people unknowingly have marched in the wrong direction... Like a smooth flow to a lake with a dangerous undercurrent. We have members of congress who are puppets of hostile power ...these shape shifting Manchurian Candidates show their double sided faces and ugly souls on TV Assassinating the characters of those who CAN make a difference... And somehow... somehow... The people refuse to vote although they know the truth.

Mandela

Because of the tribalism apartheid amongst us according to the Population Registration Act; the government has us fighting amongst one another to remain downgraded because we double the width of a natural rainbow in our color codes to the point where the vibrant Homeland Security Advisory System is fading out into pastel colored whispers over tapped phone lines …And while you were creating the clenched fist salute in midair as a trademark

Our people were busy sagging while throwing up deuces in pictures happy to be alive not standing for anything…. Leaving me to wonder just….How far the slaves have come….

Privacy is no more, freedom doesn't exist, and love is replaced by self-hate and self-sabotage Oh yes…. We can do what we want to do, go where we wish to go, So long as the perverted voyeur in big brother can watch and masturbate …

Remember when they spoke of us being tracked by aliens? Yeah well; we all have cell phones and IP addresses with GPS tracking devices that can still hear your convo even if your phone is turned off…. So…Our open door policies are involuntarily forced upon us by being SO transparent that the government has become fortune tellers of our designated fate.

During your Reflections in Prison: while you were translating Voices from the South African Liberation Struggle…Voices from Robben Island… and Pollsmoor Prison onto paper… Folks in America were getting psychotic drugs for hearing voices too and unfortunately …As of late; we have become so deconditioned to the SOS distress signals that we can only be visual with proof and with that said… HELP might come after the picture we take with our cell phones and upload to YouTube or shoot over to TMZ.

The ones with a voice that could push forward change are still shadows of the underground and are even more guarded and veiled than ever... oh yeah... back to talking about aliens among us... yeah we're past all that now... We have programs such as Fox news and Photoshop... we have democrat and republican news stations and even the anchormen could possibly be a hologram these days just so as to protect themselves from future lawsuits... our living rooms have become soup kitchens while newscasters chef up cauldrons' of false info being fed to the public...

They have created man made diseases and viruses to wipe us out, almost every generations offspring has a symptom that was Never before in our family history due to these so called mandatory vaccines ... We have medications being designed to place a worth on our life... It is with deep regret that I inform you that WE are The Tuskegee Experiment of the 21st Century.

The vortex in which we exist are a Ponzi scheme at its finest; They raised the bar and made us productive slaves to the industry dollar, as they force us into less money and more working hours and pimp us harder... Somehow subliminally convincing us that creative freedom is more precious when we are brainwashed by their thought process...

Long gone are the core hopes of the American dreams of being home and landowners ... Live in your house for 4 generations and skip your taxes and by the second quarter ....Ohhhh you'll see who owns the property for real ... We all are Prisoners in the garden

Mandela

And yet we have state to state lottery worth billions of dollars and somehow....somehow no one has money to FIX the problems..... Go figure

But... I will say that the TVs evangelists are looking kind of dapper these days for the hopeless... these type of churches have adopted the prosperity theology so there is less talk about God with over 8,000 seats in domes and atriums of willing ears and more biblically supported factually distorted incites for sowing 12 month tide commitments... Creflo Dollar was asking 29.99 and Mike Murdock is going for 58.00 so... the increase is definitely in correlation with the American obesity percentage... but belly fat is losing the race with the pocket fat of these prophets for profit...

For the past 10 years.... I have noticed that the campaigns rallying about the kids are our future hasn't been on TV either ...Reason being.... They have a taskforce force we don't see right up underneath our noses swiftly wiping them out... They are called teachers and parents who are quick to medicate and profit from the child dropping out of societies up and coming common sense regime.

And those which the magnetic talons of justice which they can't twist yet ... Are the delicious sack of soft bones which the court system gets to gnaw on by leaving tooth marked bar coded tattoos ...called a record....

All of those public promotions to put reflective decals on the windows of children rooms in case of fire... was a glow in the dark reflective bulls' eye target for intruders and just so happens to be the last window they'd go see about. ...
And let me tell you that as far as I'm concerned....the whole campaign slogan for that McGruff Safe Kids Identification Kits that was urgently pleading and

encouraging the guardians to register our child in the local police stations "just in case something happens"

… Was the ultimate Fear then Relief or rather …Scare and Convince manipulative tactic that most mechanics use. As it turns out… minority children abducted are rarely televised.

It's all a smoke screen and well; I personally wonder if they should've had a legal directory with a free calling card on the back of the ID with who to call once they locked up our children … now we got prison lottery's called indefinite detention meaning…Stop looking…

and that the dammed dog doesn't come on TV anymore…because far as I'm concerned He is in fact working with law enforcement officials undercover in a some sort of witness protection program probably looking like a pit-bull with lipstick on… I would not be surprised if he's sniffing out bombs in Newark Airport…..

You see; I too… have conversations with myself… And I have come to the conclusion that: NO CHILD LEFT BEHIND is an embellished hate code with blatant scars For NO INNOCENT will fall thru the cracks without getting marred

Radios are now considered weapons and skittles are a bag of bullets to our children …

And overnight… The whole lattice top to our warm apple pie has magically transformed into a hoody that's profusely bleeding out onto sidewalks… But no worries though….it's not a complete loss; because the wonderful high rollers called manufactures of coke cola, bleach and peroxide are negotiating deals with giving Arizona Ice Tea the same recipe to clean up the blood spills…

Mandela

Undoubtedly we all wear The Red Blanket As an aura while mourning the loss of our future leaders as the world shuffles along blissfully clueless on the anthropology of cultural diversity...

Seems that the majority; no longer care about grammar and composition. When it comes to The PLF (principle of) least effort [Zipf's Law] which has now spilled over into the indifference of ambition and have redefined shortcuts as cutting corners if it don't make dollars then it don't make sense ...

You will be missed Mandela; Thank you for the fight, we all celebrated when they finally let you out. We cheered for the bravery of your conviction when you were incarcerated and we celebrate you now as the last breadths become history books with wings... You are The Essential Series... truly a legitimate legend... Opening the eyes of sleeping masons ...saying It Is time to build.... Urging the United Nations general assembly To Invest in Peace...

I have always thought of you as the valiant warrior of revolutionary Peace & Change ... So while you are about to fall into a blissful slumber in the pillow cased arms of God ...The rest of the world needs to Wake UP because we have a lot of work to do.....

And if I could create An Unmuted Ink recognition award for you I would say: Nelson Mandela is the Poets Peace Laureate of the entire universe.....

Mandela

You are the Father Theresa in our eyes....

They say too much of anything isn't good for you ...Not even water and air....How ironic that an icon such as yourself; would die from a lung infection while still trying to inhale gulps of your freedom... it's okay to close your eyes and take flight.. So that you may finally be at eternal peace ...

Because you have indeed changed the world... And surely you and your legacy are delighted to the bone because of that...

You urged us to: Walk The Last Mile With You... My sneakers are laced up And on this 27th day of June 2013 ....we are here holding your hand with a fist pump to the sky answering your call... but for the rest of us... There is still a long walk to freedom...

Jamie Bond

Mandela

the ripple effect

humanity begins
by sticking a toe into rhetoric.
the stir creates a ripple,
in turn causing a wave.
a riptide pummels the identity into submission.
tremulous swells heighten,
blocking the fighting spirit
before society hurls all will against the rough sand
spitting out a shell,
thought ready to conform.

but a spark resides,
an ember awaiting a fan,
to kindle into a flame,
which a gale cannot extinguish.
a fire so hot,
the water steams the next time the toe dips,
leaving a warm current that people follow,
embracing the blaze,
towering as a lighthouse,
beckoning others to venture to the shallows.

droves swamp the shore,
enthralled by the notion
that the light burns brighter than the sun.
caught in the spotlight,
the identity loses sight.
media adds fuel until the land engulfs in fire.
waters churn,
heat swirls the tides,
creating a waterspout,
dowsing the brushfire,
dragging the idiom to sea.

Mandela

in turmoil,
all hope to remember the paradigm,
the inner strength,
of how one voice can make a difference,
almost dies.
the spark,
which forged others to follow,
wavers.
until looking towards land,
to behold the vision sought.
not one,
but many people,
holding hands to cross the waters,
reaching out to bridge the spark's initiative to
save humanity.

September 11, 2013

Diane Sismour

Mandela

In the words spoken by former South Africa President, Nelson Mandela, "A good head and a good heart are always a formidable combination. But when you add to that, a literate tongue or pen, then you have something very special." Individuals, as the poets and writers collaborating for the greater good, are one minded in these notions…of peace for all man, education to provide a better existence, and food for each mouth.

If motivated, a person will aspire to live in peace, progress towards better living conditions, or strive for a safer environment. Malala Yousafzai is an example of an extraordinary young woman who stood against the Taliban, and survived an attempt on her life, becoming a global voice for girls' education. She stated to an audience at Carnegie Hall, "I believe that a gun has no power at all because a gun can only kill, but a pen can live forever."

If progress moved as quickly with humane solutions as it does with electronics, imagine how much better the living environments and self-respect of individuals could be in abhorrent conditions. Where they too can fight the current and support each other, improving their world. It takes one voice, to make a conscience effort, and awaken a country. One spark to give hope when all is lost. One act of kindness, which passed forward, can grow across a land to sweep a nation. Imagine what many can do.

Diane Sismour 1/5/2014

Mandela

the vespiary

I can use

aesthetic brutality

to stir up

this vespiary

have to go back

to the middle

of the passage

the whole

the everlasting

to Egypt to Tunisia

to Uganda to Liberia

to Robben's Island blues

to Dennis Brutus

to the Tutsi

to the Hutus

to Mandela's bed

red am green

black am history

lost in translation

a colonial refugee

to Matabane to Diop

to Dakur to the King

of the court

Mandela

have to go

to the old

to the new

to the landmark

the royalty

in the jaws

of a shark

to Sahara

to Baraka

to the River

Niger

it ain't that far

far

to Kikiyu

to Twi

Kilimanjaro

to the jenjeweed

Robert Gibbons

Mandela

after Countee Cullen

" but he was dying for a dream
and he was very meek,
and his eyes there shone a gleam
men journey far to seek."

from: *Simon the Cyrenian speaks*

I did not forget my responsibility, but I am dying for a dream; it could have been any of us; quilted in the tradition of Martin or Malcolm; Mandela or Nkrumah, but I am still hear; still hearing the call of the ones who brought me; the children of muck and clay; of one thousand suns of Zora Neale Hurston; and certainly my way gets difficult; I am side-tracked; knock back to the road; the reality; to does this matter; I rather just not say; just wait until the feeling comes back to me; but in all of this, who will fight the battle; who has the shaker and the rattle; I am scrounging all week; pounding my feet against pavement; the enslavement of being invisible; only a picture on the cover of a book; it is not me; but it is spirit; the people on the other side of the river; that hide in the trees at night and guard my sleep; am nothing without them; if only I could describe plight; only cypress swamps in purple; but at the break of this day furtive; after the retreat in the mountain of memory; after the speak of tradition; another one died of arthritis or dialysis; a paralysis of the story; on their way to the city of the dreams; it is all been written down by people of God; their dreams eternal; maternal as milk on a manna breast; as stern as home made; as I walk further and further down this road.

Robert Gibbons

Mandela

his condition is unchanged
(for Nelson Mandela)

father;
I have not be circumcised
only colonized
father too,
a nation of his children
George Washington owned us
the king of the clan sold us,
but we come back
to the rhythm
we come back to the mission
his condition is unchanged
but our reason remain
we stake out Pretoria
we stake out Johannesburg
we stake out the chronic lungs
the operations and the gallstones
his fourth hospitalization
but only reparations
we stake out
a twenty-seven year imprisonment
a nineteen day treatment
we stake out Zuma
out Mthembu
we stake out
Machel and Tutu
we stake
we stake out the fires
in the ghetto
the fires in Soweto
we stake out
the father for the fatherless

Mandela

and the slaughter
for the slaughterhouse
we stake out
the sons and martyrs
fthe traders and colonizers
stake out
for Medgar and Malcolm
Martin and Trayvon
we stake out for
for the shake down
apartheid in sun city
the diamond mines
named Kimberly
we stake out
the Boers and Xhosa
we stake out
and sit in
at lunch counters
with the tongue
of the Afrikaneers
we stake out until
until Kendridge paints blood
Goldblatt captures
the bruised vagina
of Eudy Simelane
stake out Mowbray
and Table Mountain
out out out
de waterkant
out out out
Kwa Thema
Kwa Thema
Khayelitsha
Khayelitsha

Mandela

kraaforitan
Luhlaza
out
Zodwa out
Mthethwa out
stake out
out out
Banyana Banyana
out out
Miphiti
out out
Tshabalaa-Msimang
out
out
unti we live again
Hector Pieterson
shall live again
Zackie
shall live again
out stake out
until
one motherland

Robert Gibbons

AMBITION LOST

At birth we are born Chiefs, but when will we ever govern ourselves
Born soldiers, but when will we ever arm and defend ourselves
Born scholars, but when will we ever teach the knowledge of ourselves
Gifted with promise we've squandered, left lying dormant on the doormat of others

Time abused then forgotten, is time created, wasted, and rotten
Change remains the only true inevitability
How strange is a life lived without reciprocity?
Universally- Ultimately, we all get what we give
One may prosper enterprisingly
Only to fade into obscurity
A surety for ones soul- Controlled
Hot then cold
BEHOLD...
The gifts, spirit, and the call are all a given
Is it really our net worth that defines our self worth?
Is that how we are living?
A personal catastrophe lyrically expressed...
and time is real
There is no paradisaical city shinning off somewhere brightly on a hill,
but still...
Who is it that nurtures these seeds being planted?
From conception thru birth
From the time when we toddle, and waddle when we walk
Until the time comes when we are somehow melted down, and molded to our surroundings

Mandela

Surroundings encasing our very own thoughts, where we grow
Inside; or out of the "know"
Our eyes initially begin with such a brightness
speech seasoned with such exuberance
our steps blessed, and directed with such a lightness
Determined to succeed.
So, how is innocence lost?
Who's responsible for tilling the soil?
What reasoning edifies a heart that's unhealthy?
Where does knowledge begin?
and Why is ambition lost?

At birth we are born Chiefs, but when will we ever govern ourselves
Born soldiers, but when will we ever arm, and defend ourselves
Born scholars, but when will we ever teach the knowledge of ourselves?
Ambitious- One & All
Left lying dormant, on the doormat of others...

Smothered promise is squandered
Evacuated by the language of disappointment
Perceptions from the gutter, where base head mothers nurse, and care for odious lovers
Then give birth to an infant child
This child must learn to fake her smiles
Always fearful inside, but never knowing quite why
Living the lie that her mother has tied to her mind
Her innocence, and ambition side by side as they slowly die
Can you hear her cries?
Will you look her in the eyes?

Mandela

She is imitating something in theory- Eerily traversing steeple steps
on a weary trek without knowledge
Potential has never been a promise; partnered with pretense and paranoia
and sight without vision is so sure to destroy us
Like justice with no peace
an island with no beach
A sun that never sets
Frets, and fears about tomorrow
the type of serenity one must borrow
and Time Is Real...
Time wasted, then forgotten's another irretrievable bereavement
another dispossessing achievement
UN-achieved.
So how long does it take?
Do a person's yearnings somehow simply escape?
And does it take more than just blind faith?
And by nurturing this blind beast; do we indeed seal our children's fate?
My awakening...
It reveals truth
Ambition without knowledge is like a bridge half built
a bridge to nowhere
Ambition without knowledge is like a mighty battleship docked, and stranded on dry sands
Powerful; yet impotent, headed quickly nowhere
AMBITION WITHOUT KNOWLEDGE IS...
Ambition Lost. .

June Barefield

Mandela

After reading " A Long walk to freedom"; as well as some other essays, and writings from Nelson Mandela, I decided to write a poem about him specifically. After numerous attempts, and subsequent failures, I decided to take the quote that touched me so deeply, and write about it from my own perspective. Nelson has served as so many different things, for so many different groups of people, in so many varied locales. These things I was, and am still today unable to speak intelligently about; however, my struggles I know, and this is where the motivation from this piece was derived. Thank You Nelson Mandela. Rest in Power!
~JuNe

June Barefield

"Among these young men are chiefs who will never rule because we have no power to govern ourselves; soldiers who will never fight because we have no weapons to fight with; scholars who will never teach because we have no place for them to study. The abilities, the intelligence, the promise of these young men will be squandered in their futile attempts to eek out a living doing the simplest most mindless chores for the white man."

~NELSON SPEAKS of "Ambitions Lost"

Mandela

what, did you say, your name is?

neither an African nor with any other honor

yet

...

i

...

dared

...

to wait for my turn...

Sir

too many call you father brother "our leader"

i have for long been reading their proud demeanor

from the ever so negligent sidelines

cursing my whiteness along most times

i, too, have known you all my life!

spreading your word has still been a strife

ridiculed when in my native land

to the mundane most would rather clap a hand

no one could utter Xhosa even the word

Zulu or Afrikaans? nowhere to be heard

i am grateful better yet in a daze

Mandela

in disbelief of my timing of seeing these days

i beg of you imagine, Sir: Qunu

why did i deserve bunu*

i trekked ocean crests and river beds

slept in caves made tree tops my nests

doves and eagles flew with me to find my way

not even once did i go astray

tears now flood in me in red

from Sinop to Eastern Cape

what use? i am so gravely late!

...

Madiba Sir? my name?

...

hülya n yılmaz, no longer the same

*Impersonal pronoun in Turkish in the accusative case meaning "this"

Mandela

A Life of Selflessness

Beginning in 1964 . . .
Father Madiba lived nearly
3 decades behind steel bars.

Though it could not hamper
or dampen the dream
of this man
to live equally as One

banning apartheid for all
yes it was us
you and me that
he took the fall for.

Madiba, man of valor
born of royal blood
by age 71 you walked free
onto the Motherland's soil once again
the African Sun upon your face
knowing the *race* had begun
. . . once more.

In 1994 you held the office
of the 1st Black Presidency
though they tried . . .
to *crucify another King*
you held your head high
ever so gracefully.

Mandela

You, fought the battle
for respect and dignity
and they . . . yes they
tried to destroy you
but could not

it gave you more courage
to keep on marching to the beat
of your own drum, *The People's Drum*.
Thank you for daring to love
right out loud, shaking the hands
of those, your heart listening intently
to the messages, from the crowd.

We the people, are most appreciative
of you Mr. Mandela, Madiba,
Father and Grandfather
and all that you are.
A humble man, that dominated
the blood from our pounding hearts.

The many years of struggle
that is still on our minds today
though you opened many a door
to set us right . . . and on our way.

Oppression was and is our enemy
though you never exuded hate
as some might have
it was not who you were.

No bitterness, only love
from your soul did escape.
This made people awaken
and take notice.

Mandela

We love
and forever honor you . . .

Equal rights, no apartheid
looking beyond and
into our Brother's eyes.

Thank you again, for because of your courage
we dare to publicly dance together as one and sing.

Madiba

Dedicated to: Rolihlahla Mandela ~ Madiba 1918 - 2013

Janet P. Caldwell

Mandela

I vaguely remember when you were imprisoned back in 1964. I was in the 8th Grade. Kennedy and Medgar were just killed the year before. That dashed the hopes of many disenfranchised people like Myself, my Family and a Nation. We still had Martin, Robert and Malcolm amongst us though as well as Angela D., Fred Hampton, Stokely, H. Rap and Bobby Seale. Who will pick up the Torch now . . . i wonder ?

What was happening in South Africa was wrong, but it did not affect me . . .so i thought. I remember the names of Biko and Nelson's co-accused which included people that were not so familiar such as Walter Sisulu, Dennis Goldberg, Govan Mbeki, Raymond Mhlaba, Elias Mosoaledi, Andrew Mlangeni - all ANC officials and Ahmed Kathrada, the former leader of the South African Indian Congress. Yeah, i like most of my Brothers and Sisters were disconnected from any valid realities that could or would have such a profound effect on our future. I was not much on the News, and the News was not much on keeping us informed of the News. Besides, we Black Folk, Colored Folk and Negroes had our own agendas and issues we were contending with . . . daily. We were focused of such things like how to stay out of the way of "The Man" and have some fun at the same time. A decent paying job helped. And contrary to the popular lore and belief, we were not strung out on Fried Chicken and Watermelon, we ate Salads too. So much for indoctrination and the other bullshit people believe so that they may see themselves as superior. I often questioned who were the real Spear Chuckers ?

Mandela

Life was relatively good during those times of our lives even though Social unrest was nipping at our souls on many levels with Segregation, Racism, Low Paying Jobs, the Viet Nam War and of course . . . Assassinations. We were unknowingly preparing ourselves with our slumber for much unrest still yet to come. As the years eased on by we saw Malcolm, Bobby and Martin bite the dust and leave us to fend for our selves. Out in California The Panthers were representing . . . i mean like they were talking about such thing as Black Pride and Power to the People. I could relate to that. It was a proud moment when John and Carlos pumped their fist on the podium at the 1968 Summer Olympics in Mexico . . . they won but they lost. That seems to be pretty much the story for Black Folks, a saga that continues to this day. Hoses, Ropes, Bullets, Drugs, Prison and Death and more Death. But we still have our hope . . .don't we ?

This is what Nelson means to me now. I look back with my 20 / 20 hindsight and i see that he was fighting for what should have always been . . . parity, not just a chance. but Equality on all levels. How did we ever forget that we are all related and we are birthed from the same Mother? Families and Institutions such as Rhodes and Debeers further the dastardly plight and suffering of a people because of their greed as did the Dutch, Italians, French, English Crown and whoever else had a notion to. It was a low time for Humanity starting with a people who once reigned as the Kings and Queens of the Richest Land on earth. The people were exploited, enslaved, persecuted, oppressed, beaten, killed and ostracized from their civility as we see still reflected in our present day societies.

I had a pair of Platform shoes during those days. They made me feel bigger, taller, just like my Grandma 'ouise or my Aunt Bessie did when they told me how wonderful and smart i was. Those words of love and encouragement

Mandela

always made me feel better about my self and i believed that i could accomplish anything. This usually lasted until we had to ride a Bus, or enter Public Buildings separately or did not get that Job. Apartheid . . . the setting apart of our Brothers. Aren't we all created by the same God from the same source . . . Dust and Spirit ?

The struggle continues within and without as we are still set aside, such as the other side of the tracks, the other side of the room with no true honest representation of who we are in the Media, Hollywood or any other Capitalistic oriented industry. I remember such companies as Coca Cola, CitiBank, Sony and General Mills who refused to divest themselves from South Africa while we the people were in the struggle. That's right, we all are a part of the struggle, whether you know it, acknowledge it or not, regardless of what your Ethnic or Cultural persuasion is. Nelson so eloquently epitomized this when he was released from Prison. I think most people expected a Blood Bath, but he offered and proffered Peace. Many White folks didn't like that . . . we cheered. That's all we ever wanted . . Peace and Equality.

We still have yet to arrive, and the struggle does continue as is so evident every day we read the paper or turn on the news if they choose to inform the people of the truth. But we know . . . we know because of the lives of those who sacrificed their lives that we may hopefully awaken as one humanity. So without further ado, i just had to take this time to simply say to you my Brother . . . Thank You Nelson thank you Mr. Mandela, Thank You Madiba.

just bill

© 28 June 2013 : william s. peters, sr.

Mandela

i am you . . . you are me

Madiba,

you captured the saneness of the world
set aside the mess
we humans have heralded in
and accepted as
the way it should be

you walked through the gate
changed the fate
of many
who knew no better
and many
who wanted more
and many
who did not wish
to let go

the eternal River flows
in the poetry and prose
of how you lived your life
leaving behind
a legacy

Mandela

a teaching

that our strife

can be overcome

you spoke for my soul

you spoke for the whole of us

and some day

like Martin said

you said

Malcolm said

we too shall

shall see that Mountain Top

and hold our heads on high

let not our weakness draw nigh

for you and i and we

art of Sovereignty

i am you . . . you are me

just bill

© 10 February 2014 : william s. peters, sr.

Mandela

Mandela

epilogue

Mandela
the Man, His Life, Its Meaning, Our Words

Rolihlahla Nelson Mandela

July 18, 1918 ~ December 5, 2013

Mandela
the Man, His Life, Its Meaning, Our Words

Madiba

biography

Mandela
the Man, His Life, Its Meaning, Our Words

Mandela
the Man, His Life,
Its Meaning, Our Words

Rolihlahla Mandela was born into the Madiba clan in Mvezo, Transkei, on July 18, 1918, to Nonqaphi Nosekeni and Nkosi Mphakanyiswa Gadla Mandela, principal counsellor to the Acting King of the Thembu people, Jongintaba Dalindyebo.

His father died when he was a child and the young Rolihlahla became a ward of Jongintaba at the Great Place in Mqhekezweni. Hearing the elder's stories of his ancestor's valour during the wars of resistance, he dreamed also of making his own contribution to the freedom struggle of his people.

He attended primary school in Qunu where his teacher Miss Mdingane gave him the name Nelson, in accordance with the custom to give all school children "Christian" names.

He completed his Junior Certificate at Clarkebury Boarding Institute and went on to Healdtown, a Wesleyan secondary school of some repute, where he matriculated.

Nelson Mandela began his studies for a Bachelor of Arts Degree at the University College of Fort Hare but did not complete the degree there as he was expelled for joining in a student protest. He completed his BA through the University of South

Mandela
the Man, His Life, Its Meaning, Our Words

Africa and went back to Fort Hare for his graduation in 1943.

On his return to the Great Place at Mkhekezweni the King was furious and said if he didn't return to Fort Hare he would arrange wives for him and his cousin Justice. They ran away to Johannesburg instead arriving there in 1941. There he worked as a mine security officer and after meeting Walter Sisulu, an estate agent, who introduced him to Lazar Sidelsky. He then did his articles through the firm of attorneys Witkin Eidelman and Sidelsky.

Meanwhile he began studying for an LLB at the University of the Witwatersrand. By his own admission he was a poor student and left the university in 1948 without graduating. He only started studying again through the University of London and also did not complete that degree.

In 1989, while in the last months of his imprisonment, he obtained an LLB through the University of South Africa. He graduated *in absentia* at a ceremony in Cape Town.

Nelson Mandela, while increasingly politically involved from 1942, only joined the African National Congress in 1944 when he helped formed the ANC Youth League.

Mandela
the Man, His Life, Its Meaning, Our Words

In 1944 he married Walter Sisulu's cousin Evelyn Mase, a nurse. They had two sons Madiba Thembekile 'Thembi' and Makgatho and two daughters both called Makaziwe, the first of whom died in infancy. They effectively separated in 1955 and divorced in 1958.

Nelson Mandela rose through the ranks of the ANCYL and through its work the ANC adopted in 1949 a more radical mass-based policy, the Programme of Action.

In 1952 he was chosen at the National Volunteer-in-Chief of the Defiance Campaign with Maulvi Cachalia as his Deputy. This campaign of civil disobedience against six unjust laws was a joint programme between the ANC and the South African Indian Congress. He and 19 others were charged under the Suppression of Communism Act for their part in the campaign and sentenced to nine months hard labour suspended for two years.

A two-year diploma in law on top of his BA allowed Nelson Mandela to practice law and in August 1952 he and Oliver Tambo established South Africa's first black law firm, *Mandela and Tambo*.

Mandela
the Man, His Life, Its Meaning, Our Words

At the end of 1952 he was banned for the first time. As a restricted person he was only able to secretly watch as the Freedom Charter was adopted at Kliptown on 26 June 1955.

Nelson Mandela was arrested in a countrywide police swoop of 156 activists on 5 December 1955, which led to the 1956 Treason Trial. Men and women of all races found themselves in the dock in the marathon trial that only ended when the last 28 accused, including Mr. Mandela were acquitted on 29 March 1961.

On 21 March 1960 police killed 69 unarmed people in a protest at Sharpeville against the pass laws. This led to the country's first state of emergency on 31 March and the banning of the ANC and the Pan Africanist Congress on 8 April. Nelson Mandela and his colleagues in the Treason Trial were among the thousands detained during the state of emergency.

During the trial on 14 June 1958 Nelson Mandela married a social worker Winnie Madikizela. They had two daughters Zenani and Zindziswa. The couple divorced in 1996.

Mandela
the Man, His Life, Its Meaning, Our Words

Days before the end of the Treason Trial Nelson Mandela travelled to Pietermaritzburg to speak at the All-in Africa Conference, which resolved he should write to Prime Minister Verwoerd requesting a non-racial national convention, and to warn that should he not agree there would be a national strike against South Africa becoming a republic. As soon as he and his colleagues were acquitted in the Treason Trial Nelson Mandela went underground and began planning a national strike for 29, 30 and 31 March. In the face of a massive mobilization of state security the strike was called off early. In June 1961 he was asked to lead the armed struggle and helped to establish Umkhonto weSizwe (Spear of the Nation).

On 11 January 1962 using the adopted name David Motsamayi, Nelson Mandela left South Africa secretly. He travelled around Africa and visited England to gain support for the armed struggle. He received military training in Morocco and Ethiopia and returned to South Africa in July 1962. He was arrested in a police roadblock outside Howick on 5 August while returning from KwaZulu-Natal where he briefed ANC President Chief Albert Luthuli about his trip.

Mandela
the Man, His Life, Its Meaning, Our Words

He was charged with leaving the country illegally and inciting workers to strike. He was convicted and sentenced to five years imprisonment which he began serving in Pretoria Local Prison. On 27 May 1963 he was transferred to Robben Island and returned to Pretoria on 12 June. Within a month police raided a secret hide-out in Rivonia used by ANC and Communist Party activists and several of his comrades were arrested.

In October 1963 Nelson Mandela joined nine others on trial for sabotage in what became known as the Rivonia Trial. Facing the death penalty his words to the court at the end of his famous 'Speech from the Dock' on 20 April 1964 became immortalized:

"I have fought against white domination, and I have fought against black domination. I have cherished the ideal of a democratic and free society in which all persons live together in harmony and with equal opportunities. It is an ideal which I hope to live for and to achieve. But if needs be, it is an ideal for which I am prepared to die."

Mandela
the Man, His Life,
Its Meaning, Our Words

On 11 June 1964 Nelson Mandela and seven other accused Walter Sisulu, Ahmed Kathrada, Govan Mbeki, Raymond Mhlaba, Denis Goldberg, Elias Motsoaledi and Andrew Mlangeni were convicted and the next day were sentenced to life imprisonment. Denis Goldberg was sent to Pretoria Prison because he was white while the others went to Robben Island.

Nelson Mandela's mother died in 1968 and his eldest son Thembi in 1969. He was not allowed to attend their funerals.

On 31 March 1982 Nelson Mandela was transferred to Pollsmoor Prison in Cape Town with Sisulu, Mhlaba and Mlangeni. Kathrada joined them in October. When he returned to the prison in November 1985 after prostate surgery Nelson Mandela was held alone. Justice Minister Kobie Coetsee had visited him in hospital. Later Nelson Mandela initiated talks about an ultimate meeting between the apartheid government and the ANC.

In 1988 he was treated for Tuberculosis and was transferred on 7 December 1988 to a house at Victor Verster Prison near Paarl. He was released from its gates on Sunday 11 February 1990, nine days after the unbanning of the ANC and the PAC and nearly four months after the release of the

Mandela
the Man, His Life, Its Meaning, Our Words

remaining Rivonia comrades. Throughout his imprisonment he had rejected at least three conditional offers of release.

Nelson Mandela immersed himself into official talks to end white minority rule and in 1991 was elected ANC President to replace his ailing friend Oliver Tambo. In 1993 he and President FW de Klerk jointly won the Nobel Peace Prize and on 27 April 1994 he voted for the first time in his life.

On 10 May 1994 he was inaugurated South Africa's first democratically elected President. On his 80th birthday in 1998 he married Graça Machel, his third wife.

True to his promise Nelson Mandela stepped down in 1999 after one term as President. He continued to work with the Nelson Mandela Children's Fund he set up in 1995 and established the Nelson Mandela Foundation and The Mandela-Rhodes Foundation.

In April 2007 his grandson Mandla Mandela became head of the Mvezo Traditional Council at a ceremony at the Mvezo Great Place.

Mandela
the Man, His Life, Its Meaning, Our Words

Nelson Mandela never wavered in his devotion to democracy, equality and learning. Despite terrible provocation, he never answered racism with racism. His life has been an inspiration to all who are oppressed and deprived, to all who are opposed to oppression and deprivation.

Mandela
the Man, His Life, Its Meaning, Our Words

Mandela
the Man, His Life, Its Meaning, Our Words

Quotes of Madiba

Mandela
the Man, His Life, Its Meaning, Our Words

"It always seems impossible until it's done." - Nelson Mandela

"The greatest glory in living lies not in never falling, but in rising every time we fall." - Nelson Mandela

"Do not judge me by my successes, judge me by how many times I fell down and got back up again." - Nelson Mandela

"There is nothing like returning to a place that remains unchanged to find the ways in which you yourself have altered." - Nelson Mandela

"For to be free is not merely to cast off one's chains, but to live in a way that respects and enhances the freedom of others." - Nelson Mandela

"Let there be work, bread, water and salt for all." - Nelson Mandela

"A good head and good heart are always a formidable combination. But when you add to that a literate tongue or pen, then you have something very special." - Nelson Mandela

Mandela
the Man, His Life, Its Meaning, Our Words

"After climbing a great hill, one only finds that there are many more hills to climb." - Nelson Mandela

"Man's goodness is a flame that can be hidden but never extinguished" - Nelson Mandela

"When the water starts boiling it is foolish to turn off the heat." - Nelson Mandela

"Education is the most powerful weapon which you can use to change the world." - Nelson Mandela

"If you talk to a man in a language he understands, that goes to his head. If you talk to him in his language, that goes to his heart." - Nelson Mandela

"Resentment is like drinking poison and then hoping it will kill your enemies." - Nelson Mandela

"Lead from the back - and let others believe they are in front." - Nelson Mandela

"There is no passion to be found playing small - in settling for a life that is less than the one you are capable of living." - Nelson Mandela

Mandela
the Man, His Life, Its Meaning, Our Words

"If you want to make peace with your enemy, you have to work with your enemy. Then he becomes your partner." - Nelson Mandela

"No one is born hating another person because of the color of his skin, or his background, or his religion. People must learn to hate, and if they can learn to hate, they can be taught to love, for love comes more naturally to the human heart than its opposite." - Nelson Mandela

"For to be free is not merely to cast off one's chains, but to live in a way that respects and enhances the freedom of others." - Nelson Mandela

"There is no such thing as part freedom" - Nelson Mandela

"Only free men can negotiate; prisoners cannot enter into contracts. Your freedom and mine cannot be separated." - Nelson Mandela

Mandela
the Man, His Life, Its Meaning, Our Words

the Gallery

Mandela
the Man, His Life, Its Meaning, Our Words

Mandela
the Man, His Life, Its Meaning, Our Words

Mandela
the Man, His Life, Its Meaning, Our Words

Mandela
the Man, His Life,
Its Meaning, Our Words

Mandela
the Man, His Life,
Its Meaning, Our Words

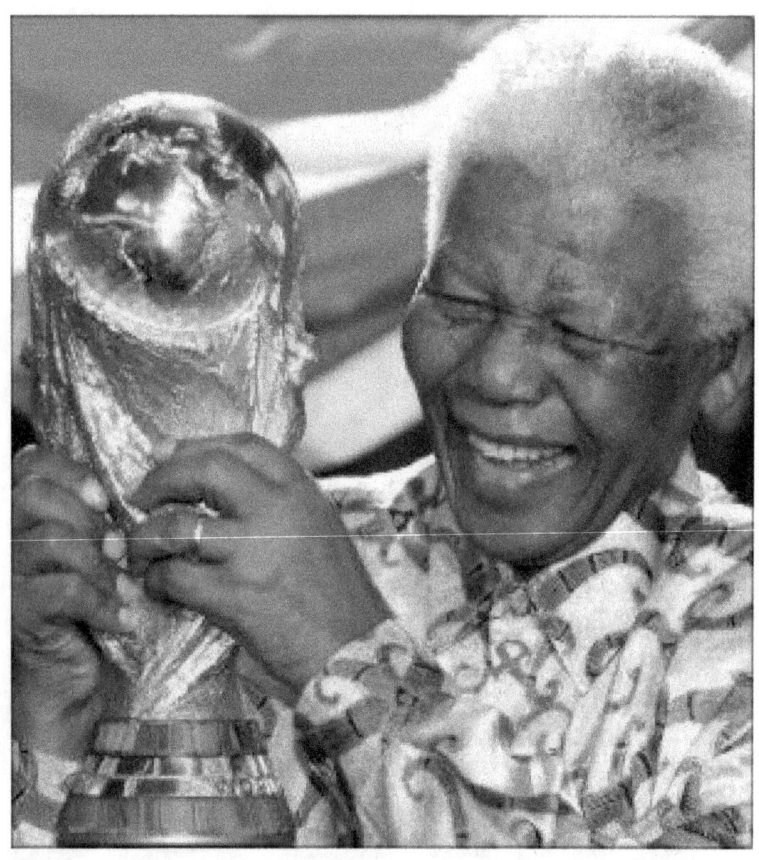

Mandela
the Man, His Life, Its Meaning, Our Words

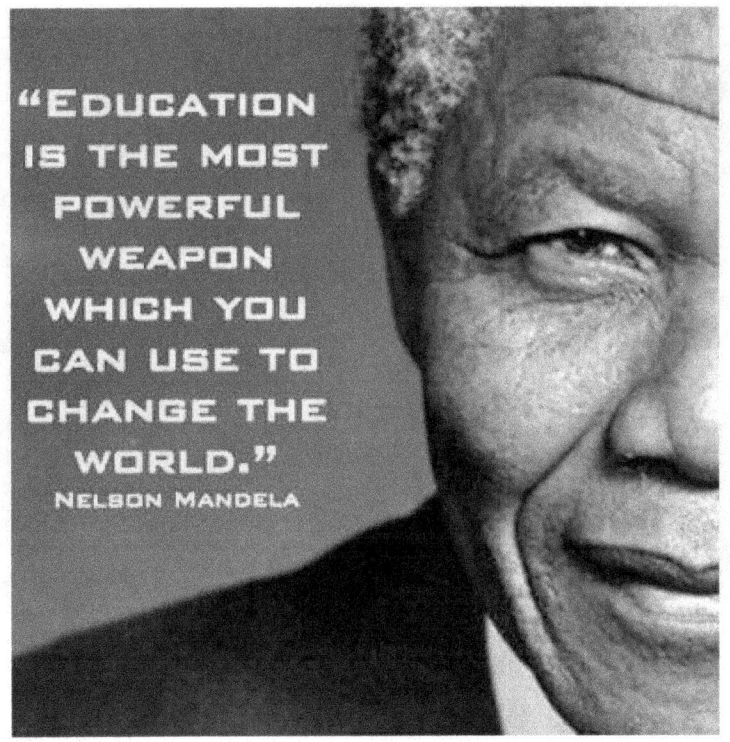

Mandela
the Man, His Life, Its Meaning, Our Words

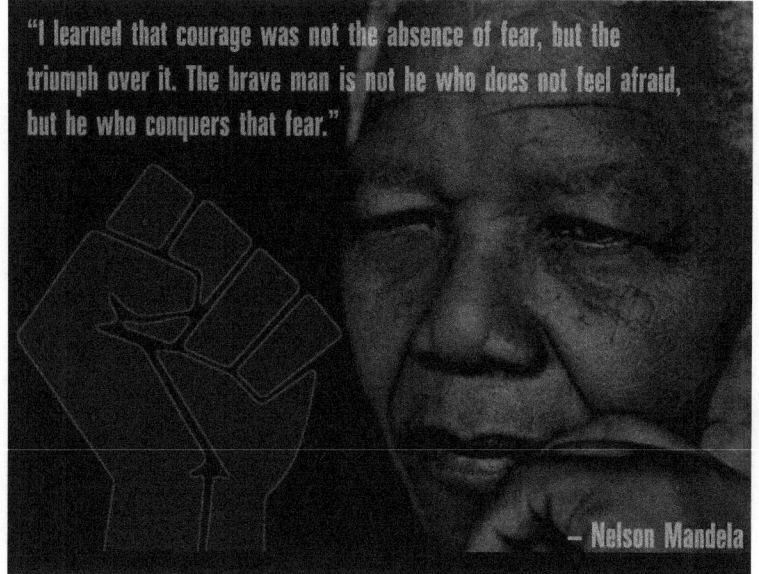

Mandela
the Man, His Life, Its Meaning, Our Words

Mandela
the Man, His Life,
Its Meaning, Our Words

Mandela
the Man, His Life, Its Meaning, Our Words

Mandela
the Man, His Life, Its Meaning, Our Words

Mandela
the Man, His Life, Its Meaning, Our Words

Mandela
the Man, His Life, Its Meaning, Our Words

Mandela
the Man, His Life, Its Meaning, Our Words

Mandela
the Man, His Life,
Its Meaning, Our Words

Mandela
the Man, His Life,
Its Meaning, Our Words

Mandela
the Man, His Life,
Its Meaning, Our Words

Mandela
the Man, His Life, Its Meaning, Our Words

Mandela
the Man, His Life, Its Meaning, Our Words

Mandela
the Man, His Life, Its Meaning, Our Words

Mandela
the Man, His Life,
Its Meaning, Our Words

Mandela
the Man, His Life, Its Meaning, Our Words

This Anthological Publication
is underwritten solely by

Inner Child Press

Inner Child Press is a Publishing Company Founded and Operated by Writers. Our personal publishing experiences provides us an intimate understanding of the sometimes daunting challenges Writers, New and Seasoned may face in the Business of Publishing and Marketing their Creative "Written Work".

For more Information

Inner Child Press

www.innerchildpress.com

a few other

Anthologies

of

Inner Child Press

for a FULL listing visit

http://www.innerchildpress.com/anthologies-sales-special.php

World Healing World Peace

A POETRY ANTHOLOGY
Volume 1

World Healing World Peace

A POETRY ANTHOLOGY
Volume 2

A GATHERING OF WORDS

POETRY & COMMENTARY
FOR
TRAYVON MARTIN

for a FULL listing visit

http://www.innerchildpress.com/anthologies-sales-special.php

www.innerchildpress.com

~ * ~

Inner Child Press, ltd.

an Inner Child Enterprises Company

www.iaminnerchild.com

www.ingramcontent.com/pod-product-compliance
Lightning Source LLC
Chambersburg PA
CBHW061656040426
42446CB00010B/1766